# YURI GAGARIN
## The First Spaceman

Written and Illustrated by

Vix Southgate

Additional resources can be found at:

www.vixsouthgate.co.uk/resources

Please note: All external links have been chosen for their child-friendly content, however they are not monitored regularly. vixsouthgate.co.uk is not responsible for the content of any website other than its own.

It is recommended that children are supervised while using the internet.

Sponsored by:

for the 50th Anniversary

With thanks to:

The British Council, RIA Novosti, The Reading Agency, YuriGagarin50.org, Canterbury University, Simple Web Design, The Attic Room, The Science Museum, Hulton Archives, Spaced Design, Barlborough Hall School, and friends and family for their support.

First Edition.

# Contents

# Yuri's Story

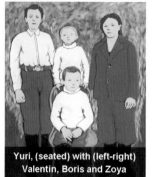

Yuri, (seated) with (left-right) Valentin, Boris and Zoya

Yuri Alexeyevich Gagarin was born on 9th March 1934 in a village called Klushino, near Gzhatsk in the Soviet Union *(now known as Russia)*. He had two brothers, Valentin and Boris and a sister, Zoya.

Their father, Alexei, was a carpenter and worked on a farm maintaining the buildings and hoped, one day, to pass his woodworking skills on to his sons. Their mother, Anna, who was born in St Petersburg, worked on the farm as a dairymaid.

Yuri attended the local school, but when the German Army invaded in 1941 all the schools were closed. He did not have any education for two years. When he was seven years old his village was captured and the Gagarins' house was taken over by the German soldiers. This meant that they had to dig themselves a shelter to live in. It was nothing more than a mud hut in their garden.

Yuri the Schoolboy

**Fact**
*Gzhatsk was renamed Gagarin in 1968.*

The Germans were driven out of the nearby town of Gzhatsk on 9th April 1943 and soon after, Klushino was also liberated.

The family salvaged what was left of their home and rebuilt it in Gzhatsk. In early 1943 the Germans had taken Yuri's eldest brother, Valentin, and his sister, Zoya, to work in labour camps in Poland and even though they escaped, they did not return home until after the war in 1945.

**Fact**
*In 1934 Russia was part of the Soviet Union and was a Communist state, led by Joseph Stalin.*

For over a year they were drafted into the Soviet Army, Valentin was sent to fight on the front-line, and Zoya, aged only 15, was put to work with the cavalry horses.

After the war, Yuri went back to school and with the help of volunteer teachers he was able to catch up with his education. Valentin trained to be a carpenter and helped rebuild the villages that had been destroyed during the war. Yuri did not want to be a carpenter or stay in the countryside; he wanted to carry on learning, even if it meant going against his family's wishes. So aged only 15, Yuri left home and went to live with an Uncle in Moscow. He was accepted into the Lyubertsy School, which was a technical high school attached to a steel works, and began learning to be a foundryman (metal-worker).

Yuri the Foundryman

*Fact* A foundryman is someone that works in a foundry - steel works - a place that casts metal.

Yuri and a YAK-18

In 1951, after graduating from Lyubertsy, he enrolled at Saratov Industrial School on a four year foundry course. In 1955 he graduated as a moulder, with very good marks.

During his time at the Industrial School, Yuri had joined The Saratov Aero Club where he spent all his spare time and learned to fly light aircraft. The first plane he flew was the YAK-18.

He impressed his instructor so much, with his discipline, dedication and passion for flying, that he was recommended for the Orenburg Military Aviation School. This success and recognition, along with his childhood passion for aeroplanes, changed the course of his life from that of a qualified caster-moulder to signing up to be a pilot in the Soviet Air Force in 1956.

Yuri the Cadet

Yuri, Valentina, Galina and Elena

It was during his first year at Orenburg that Yuri met Valentina Goryacheva, a student nurse on the base. They met at a dance on the airbase and married a year later on 27th October 1957.

On 4th October 1957 the Soviets successfully launched the world's first artificial satellite into orbit.

This satellite was called SPUTNIK.

The success of Sputnik-1 meant that on 3rd November 1957 Sputnik-2 was launched. On board was a dog named Laika, who became the first dog in space. This proved spaceflight was possible and they went on to develop and test the spacecraft that would eventually take a human into orbit.

The SPUTNIK satellite

The Space Race was on!

Yuri graduated from the Orenburg flight school on 6th November 1957 and was posted as a Lieutenant to the Nikel Airbase in Luostari in Murmansk, near the Arctic Circle, where, in April 1959, Valentina gave birth to their first daughter Elena.

*Fact*

*Sputnik-1 burned up on 4 January 1958, as it fell from orbit after travelling about 60 million km (37 million miles) and spending 3 months in orbit.*

In the October of 1959 a secret recruitment team arrived at the airbase. Thousands of men were interviewed, 154 of whom were

*Fact*

*A cosmonaut is what the Russians call an astronaut.*

tested but only 20 were put through for more training. Yuri was one of them. He and 19 others went on for special training at a purpose-built site called Star City in Moscow.

On 11th January 1960. Yuri, aged 26, began his cosmonaut training. He was training to go into space. This was the first part of the Vostok Programme - Vostok-1. The training was extremely hard and tested him beyond the limits of many men.

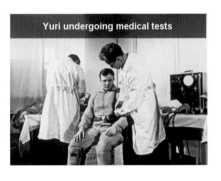
Yuri undergoing medical tests

Medical scientists did all kinds of tests to make sure that, if he was the one chosen for the mission, he was strong enough to withstand the force of the flight and mentally able to cope with the loneliness and confines of a small space capsule.

Although Yuri was a pilot, he was not expected to fly the spacecraft. Unlike today's spacecraft, Vostok-1 was controlled by people on the ground because, at that time, nobody knew how flying in space would affect his reactions and abilities.

Belka and Strelka

Throughout 1960 the Soviet space programme continued to test its capsules and ejector seat systems, making sure they were safe enough for a human passenger. On 19th August 1960 two dogs called Belka and Strelka, were launched into space.

They became the world's first dogs to go into orbit and come back unharmed. This success meant that the Soviets were one step closer to sending a human into space. All this was achieved under the watchful eye of The Chief Designer. Yuri met The Chief Designer for the first time in June 1960. Over the following months he became Yuri's mentor and a very good friend.

*Fact* Belka and Strelka were successfully launched and retrieved from orbit on board Sputnik-5, a prototype of the Vostok spacecraft that would carry Yuri into space.

Sergei Pavlovich Korolëv

Gagarin and Korolëv

The Chief Designer was in charge of the design and development of all the Soviet space missions and oversaw the Sputnik and Vostok Programmes.

The Chief Designer was never called by his real name because it was feared, that if his identity was known, he might be kidnapped for his knowledge. So, for his own safety, his true identity was kept a secret until his death in 1966. The Soviet people also knew him as 'The Father of the Soviet Space Program'.

His real name was Sergei Pavlovich Korolëv.

Korolëv was born on 12th January 1907 and trained as an aircraft designer until 1944, when he became a rocket designer. He led a team of engineers to develop the world's first intercontinental ballistic missile, known in Russia as the R-7. He was put in charge of the Soviet Space Programme and his R-7 missile design was used to launch many

R-7 rocket launch - Vostok-1

missions into space, including Sputnik-1 and Yuri's Vostok-1. Korolëv adapted his designs so that the rocket could carry more people and heavier loads into space. He also designed the Soyuz rockets which are still used today.

Sergei Korolëv's achievements include: the first satellite in space; the first animal in space; the first man in space; the first woman in space; the first three-person mission; the first spacewalk.

Korolëv died on 14th January 1966, 10 months before the launch of the first unmanned Soyuz mission. The Soyuz is still considered the world's safest human spaceflight system and has taken tourists into space.

Yuri the Cosmonaut

The dummy was amusingly named Ivan Ivanovich.

On 25th March 1961, less than a month before Yuri's historic flight, a dog called Zvëzdochka ('Little Star') - named by Yuri, made a single orbit on board Sputnik 10 with a cosmonaut dummy. To test the seat ejection system the dummy was ejected out of the capsule while Zvëvdochka stayed inside. This meant that the Vostok Programme was ready to send a human into space. From the 20 cosmonauts selected, Yuri Gagarin and Gherman Titov were chosen for the mission but it wasn't known until two days before the launch which one of them would fly.

Yuri's wife, Valentina, gave birth to their second daughter, Galina, on 7th March and the day after bringing them back from the hospital, Yuri left for Baikonur with Gherman for the final part of their training.

Yuri and Titov on the way to Baikonur

It was confirmed on 10th April that Yuri would be the first man in space and Gherman Titov would be his back-up. The next day they went to a cottage on the edge of the launch base. They took more tests to make sure they were both healthy enough to fly.  For their last lunch before the flight, they ate 'space food' which was two servings of meat purée and one of chocolate sauce, eaten out of  toothpaste-like tubes.

Gherman Titov became the second man to orbit the Earth and the first human to sleep in space and to suffer from 'space sickness' (motion sickness in space). Aged only 25 years old at launch, he remains the youngest person to fly in space.

In the evening Korolëv visited the cottage to wish them a good night and then he went to check on the launch preparations. Yuri and Gherman talked to each other in the dark before they rested for the night.

The ë is pronounced 'yo'. Zvëzdochka is pronounced Zvyozdochka

On 12th April 1961 Yuri Gagarin boarded his rocket and became the first human to orbit the Earth, on board Vostok-1.

Yuri's words to his nation before he travelled into space were:

Sergei Korolëv saying farewell to Yuri

*"Dear friends, known and unknown, fellow citizens and people of the world. In a few minutes a mighty spaceship will carry me off into the distant spaces of the universe. What can I say to you during these last minutes before the start? All my life now, seems as a single beautiful moment to me; All I have done and lived for, has been done and lived for this moment. It is difficult for me to analyse my feelings now that the hour of trial for which we have prepared so long and passionately, is so near. It's hardly worth talking about the feelings I experienced when I was asked to make this first space flight in history. Joy? No, it was not only joy. Pride? No, it was not only pride. I was immensely happy to be the first in outer space, to meet nature face to face in this unusual single-handed encounter. Could I possibly have dreamed of more? Then I thought of the tremendous responsibility I had taken on: To be the first to accomplish what generations of people dreamed of: To be the first to pave the way for humanity to outer space. Can you name a more complex task than the one I am undertaking? This is a responsibility, not to one, not to many, and not to a collective group. This is a responsibility to all the Soviet people, to all of humanity, to its present and future. I know I have to summon all my will power to carry out my assignment to the best of my ability. I understand the importance of my mission and shall do all I can to fulfil the assignment for the Communist party and the Soviet people.*

*Only a few minutes are left before the start. I am saying good-bye to you, dear friends as people always say good-bye to each other when leaving on a long journey."*

**Fact**

*Before boarding, Yuri needed a wee, so he went on the nearest available object. It is now a tradition for all cosmonauts, to urinate on the back tyre of the transport bus before their flights.*

The countdown begins.

A 27 year old Soviet pilot called Yuri Gagarin is in the Vostok-1 spacecraft on the Baikonur launch pad.

The Vostok-1 rocket is launched into space.

Fact

*Zarya was the code name for the launch site and Kedr (Cedar) was Yuri Gagarin's name during the mission.*

The strap-on booster sections shut down and drop away and the nose fairing releases.

06:09

The rocket core stage shuts down and falls away from the spacecraft.

The spacecraft is still firing; pushing Vostok-1 and Yuri toward orbit.

Vostok-1 starts to pass over Yuri's homeland, Russia.

Yuri begins to lose radio contact with ground control as Vostok-1 moves out of radio range.

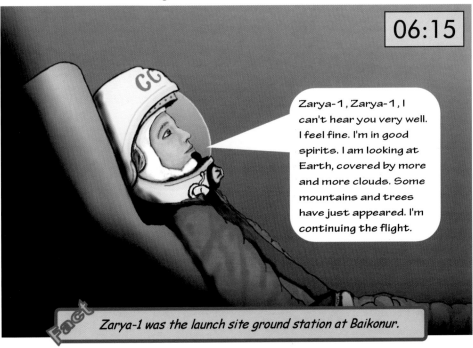

The final stages shut down. The spacecraft separates.
Vostok-1 and Yuri reach orbit.

Yuri can see the North Pacific Ocean.

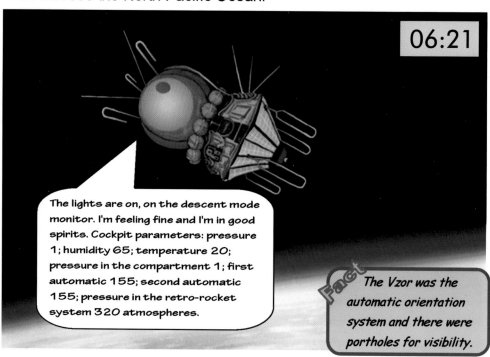

After only six minutes in orbit Yuri asks for his orbital parameters.

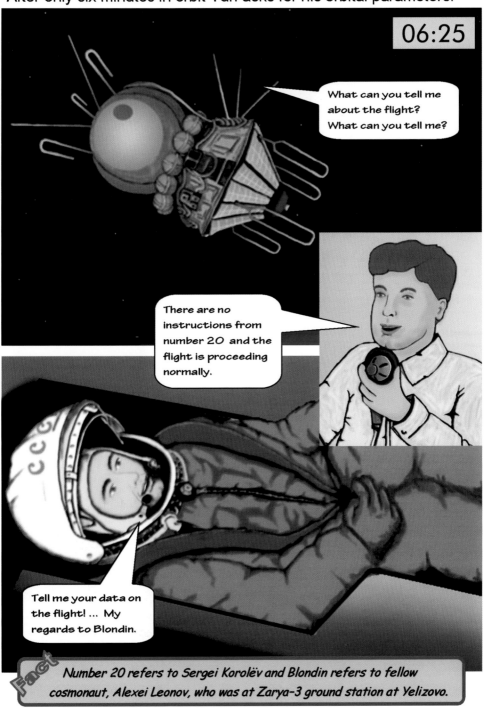

Yuri is nearly out of radio range, reaching the VHF radio horizon.

Vostok-1 moves out of VHF range and contact is lost.

Vostok-1 crosses the equator. Yuri sends his status report by HF radio.

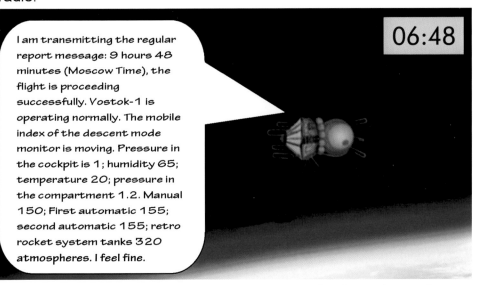

Yuri reports he is on the night side of Earth and a few minutes later he switches on the sun seeking altitude control system.

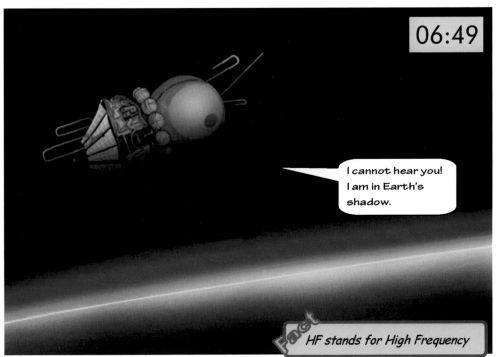

The Khabarovsk ground station tells Yuri that Vostok-1 is in a stable orbit.

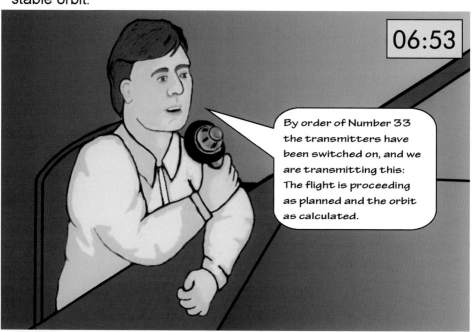

06:53

By order of Number 33 the transmitters have been switched on, and we are transmitting this: The flight is proceeding as planned and the orbit as calculated.

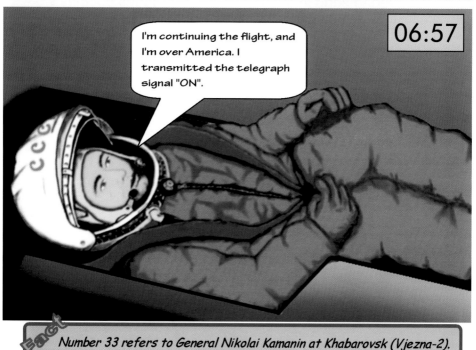

06:57

I'm continuing the flight, and I'm over America. I transmitted the telegraph signal "ON".

Fact

*Number 33 refers to General Nikolai Kamanin at Khabarovsk (Vjezna-2).*

Vostok-1 passes over the South Pacific between New Zealand and Chile and news of the Vostok mission is broadcast on Radio Moscow.

Yuri attempted to send spacecraft status messages but they were not received by ground stations.

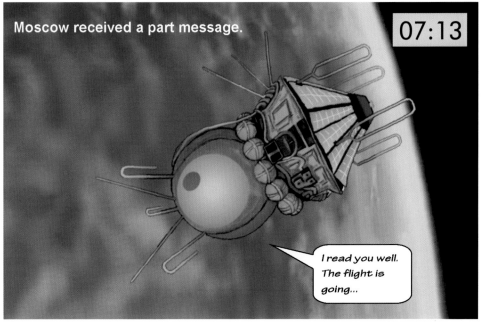

Vostok-1's retros are fired for 42 seconds.

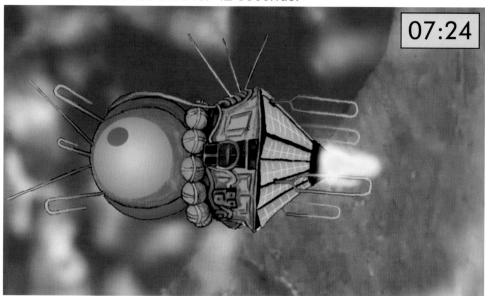

07:24

Ten seconds after retrofire, commands are sent to separate the Vostok service module from the re-entry module.

They fail to release for another 10 minutes.

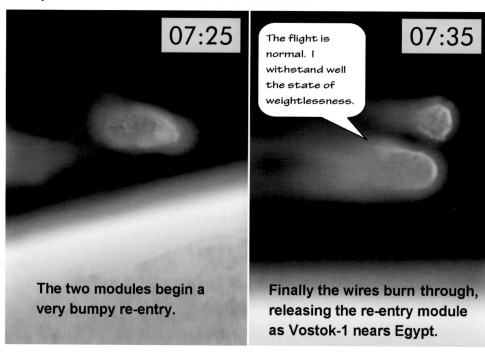

07:25

07:35

The flight is normal. I withstand well the state of weightlessness.

The two modules begin a very bumpy re-entry.

Finally the wires burn through, releasing the re-entry module as Vostok-1 nears Egypt.

Vostok-1 is 7km from the ground. Vostok-1's main parachute is deployed. Yuri's hatch is released and he ejects. 07:55

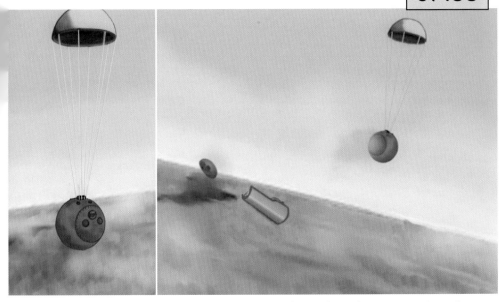

The Vostok capsule lands. Yuri jumps from the ejector seat and deploys his parachute.

Yuri Gagarin lands 10 minutes after his spacecraft. Anna Takhtarova and her granddaughter Rita were the first to see the orange suited spaceman.

Yuri wore the SK-1 Sokol (falcon) spacesuit during his flight.

Still from the film 'The First Trip to the Stars'

On April 12th 1961, at 07:55 UTC (10:55 Moscow time) after an epic journey lasting 108 minutes, including just over 89 minutes in orbit, the Soviet Union made a radio announcement telling the nation, that Yuri Gagarin had landed safely.

Yuri's space flight made him a national hero and worldwide celebrity. His first world tour to promote the Soviet achievement included visits to Czechoslovakia, Bulgaria, Finland, The United Kingdom, Iceland, Cuba, Brazil, Canada and Hungary.

**Fact** *Yuri's spacecraft reached speeds exceeding 27,000 kilometres per hour; which was three times faster than any person had flown before.*

The ё is pronounced 'yo'. Serëgin is pronounced Seryogin

In the September of 1961, after completing his first tour, Yuri Gagarin joined the Air force Engineering Academy (VVIA).

Over the years, Yuri worked on several space missions and trained other cosmonauts but was banned from flying. He was finally allowed to re-enter the mission programme in 1965 as a back-up cosmonaut for the first Soyuz flight. Unfortunately Yuri did not travel in space again, nor did he live to see a man walk on the moon in 1969.

Colonel Yuri Alexeyevich Gagarin died on 27th March 1968. He was on a routine test flight in a MiG-15 UTI when it crashed killing him and his co-pilot, Colonel Vladimir Serëgin. Their funeral took place on 30th March and their remains are buried in the Kremlin wall in Moscow.

Yuri Alexeyevich Gagarin

# Yuri facts

* Yuri's full name was: Yuri Alexeyevich Gagarin.

* Gagarin was 1.57 metres (5ft 2in) tall.

* When he was a boy, Yuri read books by Jules Verne.

* Yuri wanted to be a gymnast.

* Yuri only flew in one space mission, Vostok-1.

* Yuri was a keen ice hockey player.

* He was also a basketball fan, and coached the Saratov Industrial Technical School team, as well as being an umpire/referee.

* He was eventually offered a place at a physical training technical school to pursue his gymnastic ambitions but chose to continue as a foundryman in Saratov.

* A crater on the far side of our moon is named after him.

* Virgin trains have named one of their Super Voyager diesel-electric railcars after him.

* Yuri's ashes are buried in the Kremlin Wall.

# Flight Card

| | | | |
|---|---|---|---|
| Comonaut: | **Yuri Alexeyevich Gagarin** | Date: | **12th April 1961** |
| Age: | **27** | Launch Time: | **06:07 UTC** |
| Launch Site: | **Baikonur Cosmodrome** | Flight Duration: | **108 mins** |
| Mission: | **VOSTOK-1** | Speed: | **27,400 km per hr** |
| Spacecraft: | **VOSTOK 3KA** | Height: | **327 km above earth** |

# Russian Rockets

In 1945 Sergei Korolëv went on a reconnaissance mission into German territory to recover the V-2 rocket technology. After reproducing lost documentation and studying various parts of the V-2 rockets, the Soviets developed the first intercontinental ballistic missile. The most notable of these is known in Russia as the R-7. The R-7 was used for decades as the main launch rocket for the Soviet missions. The N-1, which is a modified R-7, is still used today to launch the Soyuz.

## The Sputnik Programme

The Sputnik programme is the commonly known name of a group of various robotic spacecraft missions launched by the Soviet Union.

The first of these, *Sputnik-1*, launched the first man-made object (an artificial satellite) into Earth orbit.

## The Vostok Programme

The Vostok programme was a Soviet human spaceflight project that succeeded in putting a person into Earth orbit for the first time.

## The Voskhod Programme

The Voskhod programme was a Soviet human spaceflight project. Voskhod development was a follow-on to the Vostok programme and a recycling of components left over from the Vostok programme's cancellation.

Voskhod-1 was the first space flight to carry more than one crewman into outer space.

## The Soyuz (spacecraft)

The Soyuz spacecraft was designed for the Soviet space programme by the Korolëv Design Bureau in the 1960s, and is still in service today. The Soyuz succeeded the Voskhod spacecraft and was originally built as part of the Soviet manned lunar programme.

# Russian Firsts
## 1957 - 1966

**1957**
* First intercontinental ballistic missile. R-7 Semyorka.
* First satellite. Sputnik-1.
* First animal in Earth orbit. Laika the dog, Sputnik-2.

**1959**
* First rocket ignition in Earth orbit. Luna-1.
* First man-made object to escape Earth's gravity. Luna-1.
* First data communications (telemetry) to and from outer space. Luna-1.
* First man-made object to pass near the Moon. Luna-1.
* First man-made object in Heliocentric orbit. Luna-1.
* First probe to impact the Moon. Luna-2.
* First images of the Moon's far side. Luna-3.

**1960**
* First animals to safely return from Earth orbit. The dogs, Belka and Strelka, Sputnik-5.

**1961**
* First probe launched to Venus. Venera-1.
* First person in space and in Earth orbit. Yuri Gagarin. Vostok-1. Vostok programme.
* First person to spend over 24 hours in space. Gherman Titov. Vostok-2 (also first person to sleep in space and feel space sickness).

**1962**
* First dual-manned spaceflight. Vostok-3.
* First probe launched to Mars. Mars-1.

**1963**
* First woman in space. Valentina Tereshkova. Vostok-6.

**1964**
* First multi-person crew (3). Voskhod-1.

**1965**
* First spacewalk. Alexsei Leonov. Voskhod-2.
* First probe to hit another planet of the Solar system (Venus). Venera-3

**1966**
* First probe to make a soft landing on and transmit from the surface of the moon. Luna-9.
* First probe in lunar orbit. Luna-10.

# Russian Firsts
## 1967 - Present Day

**1967**
* First unmanned rendezvous and docking between two spacecraft. Cosmos 186 and Cosmos 188.
(Until 2006, this was the only major space achievement that the US had not duplicated.)

**1969**
* First docking between two manned craft in Earth orbit and exchange of crews. Soyuz-4 and Soyuz-5.

**1970**
* First soil samples extracted automatically and returned to Earth. Luna-16.
* First robotic space rover. Lunokhod-1 on the Moon.
* First data received from the surface of another planet of the Solar system (Venus). Venera-7.

**1971**
* First space station. Salyut-1.
* First probe to reach the surface. Mars-2.
* First to make a soft landing on Mars. Mars-2.

**1975**
* First probe to orbit Venus. Venera-9.
* First to make a soft landing on Venus. Venera-9.
* First photos from the surface of Venus. Venera-9.

**1984**
* First woman to walk in space. Svetlana Savitskaya. Salyut-7 space station.

**1986**
* First crew to visit two separate space stations. Mir and Salyut -7.
* First probes to deploy (release) robotic balloons into Venus's atmosphere and return pictures of a comet during close flyby. Vega-1 and Vega-2.
* First permanently manned space station, Mir, 1986–2001.

**1987**
* First crew to spend over one year in space. Vladimir Titov and Musa Manarov. Soyuz TM-4 - Mir.

**1988 - Present Day**
Russia, The United States, The United Kingdom and many other countries have contributed technology and resources to enable the human race to continue to probe even deeper into the wonders of the universe and develop space travel.

# Timeline of Yuri Gagarin's life
## 1934 - 1955

| | | |
|---|---|---|
| 09 March 1934 | Yuri Alexeyevich Gagarin born | Klushino, nr Gzhatsk (Smolensk region) |
| 1941 | Enrols in a Grade School | Klushino |
| Spring 1941 | Germany attacks The Soviet Union | USSR |
| October 1942 | Klushino attacked and occupied by Germans | Klushino |
| Spring 1943 | Valentin and Zoya abducted | |
| 09 April 1943 | Germans retreat from Gzhatsk | Klushino |
| Autumn 1945 | Valentin and Zoya return home | Klushino |
| 1946 | Inspired by ex-airman teacher | Gzhatsk |
| Summer 1949 | Finishes secondary school (6th grade)<br>Moves in with an Uncle | Gzhatsk<br>Moscow |
| 30 September 1949 | Starts at Vocational School no.10<br>(Training as a foundry-man) | Lyubertsy, Moscow |
| Summer 1951 | Graduates from Vocational School no.10 | Lyubertsy, Moscow |
| September 1951 | Starts at Saratov Industrial Technical School | Saratov, Moscow |
| 04 September 1954 | Starts at Saratov Oblast Flying Club | Saratov, Moscow |
| 14 March 1955 | First parachute jump | Saratov, Moscow |
| September 1955 | Drafted into Orenburg Flying School | Orenburg |
| November 1955 | Rank: CADET | Orenburg |
| 22 February 1956 | Rank: CADET SERGEANT - permitted to fly | Orenburg |

# Timeline of Yuri Gagarin's life
## 1956 - 1961

| | | |
|---|---|---|
| October 1956 | Meets Valentina Goryacheva | Orenburg |
| 26 March 1957 | First Solo Flight in MiG-15 jet | Orenburg |
| 04 October 1957 | SPUTNIK launched | |
| 27 October 1957 | Marries Valentina Goryacheva | Orenburg |
| November 1957 | Graduates from Military School | Orenburg |
| | Posted as LIEUTENANT in Soviet Air Force | Luostari, Murmansk |
| 10 April 1959 | Elena Gagarina born | Luostari, Murmansk |
| 05 October 1959 | Tested for Cosmonaut training | Luostari, Murmansk |
| 06 November 1959 | Rank: FIRST LIEUTENANT | Luostari, Murmansk |
| 11 January 1960 | Approved for cosmonaut training | Star City, Moscow |
| 18 June 1960 | Meets Sergei Korolëv | Star City, Moscow |
| 07 March 1961 | Galina Gagarina born | Gzhatsk |
| 06 January 1961 | Yuri Gagarin and Gherman Titov selected | Star City, Moscow |
| 16 March 1961 | Sent to Tyuratam for final training | Tyuratam, Baikonur |
| 10 April 1961 | Officially confirmed for launch | Tyuratam, Baikonur |
| **12 April 1961** | **YURI GAGARIN ORBITS THE EARTH** | **Tyuratam, Baikonur** |
| 12 April 1961 | Rank: MAJOR | In Orbit |
| 14 April 1961 | Received as a hero in Moscow | Moscow |
| 18 April 1961 | Undergoes 6 days of observation | Star City, Moscow |

# Timeline of Yuri Gagarin's life
## 1961 - 1968

| | | |
|---|---|---|
| 21 April 1961 | Appears on the cover of TIME Magazine | United States |
| 25 April 1961 | Begins his World Tour | Global |
| April - August 1961 | World tour | Czechoslovakia, Bulgaria, Finland, UK, Iceland, Poland, Cuba, Brazil, Canada and Hungary |
| 01 September 1961 | Starts at the Air Force Engineering Academy | Zhukovsky |
| 29 November - 15 December 1961 | Asian Tour | India, Sri Lanka, Afganistan |
| 12 June 1962 | Rank: LIEUTENANT COLONEL | Zhukovsky |
| September 1963 | State visit to France | Paris |
| 06 November 1963 | Rank: COLONEL | Zhukovsky |
| April 1965 | Re-enters mission training as a back-up cosmonaut | Zhukovsky |
| September 1965 | Starts at the Institute of Aeronautical Engineering | Zhukovsky |
| 1967 | Begins training as a back-up for the first manned Soyuz flight | Zhukovsky |
| 17 February 1968 | Graduates with honours as cosmonaut engineer | Zhukovsky |
| 27 March 1968 | Death of Colonel Yuri Alexeyevich Gagarin<br><br>Crash lands in a MiG-15UTI alongside Colonel Vladimir Serëgin | Kirzhach |

# Information Sources

## Books

Starman - James Doran & Piers Bizony      ISBN 0-7475-3688-0

One Small Step - David Whitehouse      ISBN 978-1-84866-036-6

My Brother Yuri - Valentin Gagarin

Road to the Stars - Yuri Gagarin

Soviet Man in Space - Yuri Gagarin

## Website resources:

www.vixsouthgate.co.uk

www.yurigagarin50.org

www.rtc.ru/encyk/gagarin/main1.shtml (in Russian)

www.astronautix.com/astros/gagarin.htm

www.en.wikipedia.org/wiki/Yuri_Gagarin

www.russianspaceweb.com/vostok1.html

www.russianarchives.com/gallery/gagarin/

www.en.wikipedia.org/wiki/Sputnik_program

www.en.wikipedia.org/wiki/Vostok_programme

www.en.wikipedia.org/wiki/Voskhod_programme

www.en.wikipedia.org/wiki/Soyuz_(spacecraft)

www.footagevault.com

www.spaced-out.biz

All images courtesy of RIA Novosti      http://visualrian.com

For RIA Novosti image enquires please contact:      photos@novosti.co.uk

This book is sponsored by:

 and supported by:

*Original 1961 poster, courtesy of Steve Moore Cinema Poster Archive.*

Newsreels 1-3 of 'With Gagarin to the Stars'

are available at:

http://www.britishpathe.com/

*Russian with an English commentary available (English audio missing on reel 3)*